Meles and the Ferocious Farmer

Also by Dr Colin Bonnington

The Grey Tale of Mrs Sciurus

Meles and the Ferocious Farmer

by Dr Colin Bonnington

First published in 2018 by Dr Colin Bonnington

Illustrations copyright © Colin Bonnington
Front and back covers designed by Chris Freeman

ISBN 978-1-9999394-1-0

All rights reserved. No part of this book may be reproduced, stored in a retrieval system, or transmitted in any form, or by any means, electronic, mechanical, photocopying, recording or otherwise, without prior written permission from the publisher.

A catalogue record of this book is available from the British Library.

Any resemblance to persons fictional or real, living or dead, is purely coincidental.

For my wife Suz and bump

Chapter 1
A Reluctant Farmer

Do you know anyone who doesn't like animals?

You might know someone who says, 'I don't like cats' or 'I'm not keen on dogs.' But do you know anyone who doesn't like any animals at all?

Well, meet Farmer Buck. I would say that he's pleased to meet you, but he's not. And that beside him is his dog, Mr Scruff.

Yes, I know what you're about to say. 'But you just said that Farmer Buck doesn't like any animals.' Well, you see, Farmer Buck doesn't, and that's why he called his terrier Mr Scruff - because he sees his canine companion as more of a person than a dog. A four-legged, hairy and stinky person, but a person nonetheless.

Isn't he small, slight and wiry? Just look at those shifty eyes and that wet nose. And what about the dog, Mr Scruff?! They're like two peas in a pod, don't you think?

Now, not only do Farmer Buck and Mr Scruff look alike, but they also have similar qualities. Actually, it's not qualities at all. Personalities - that's more like it. Both are as stubborn as a stoat, as horrible as a hound, and as selfish as a shellfish.

And these two here are Farmer Buck's terrible twin boys, Pete and Paul.

Although they aren't identical, they look roughly the same. That's Pete on the left and Paul on the right. At least, I think it is. Pete is nine years old and Paul is the same. Both boys are already much taller than their father. Pete and Paul hate animals as much as one another, and maybe even more than Farmer Buck. So, if you're an animal you'd be best advised to keep away from the Bucks and their home, Cuckoo Nest Farm. However, it wasn't always like this.

Farmer Buck's own father had been a nice, cheery chap. Such niceness had obviously not been passed down the generations. Farmer Buck Senior had lived at Cuckoo Nest Farm and he had liked all animals, of all shapes and sizes, domestic or wild. He kept a small herd of cows, a family of pigs and a gaggle of geese. He also used to put food out for the wild animals: seed for the birds, cat food for the hedgehogs and peanuts for the badgers. However, Buck Senior had retired and the farm had come to his only son, Farmer Buck. (You must excuse me, but I don't know his name. Come to think of it, I don't think anyone does; he hasn't told anyone).

Farmer Buck at least waited until his frail old father had snuffed it before he went about single-handedly destroying all that he had built at Cuckoo Nest Farm. All the cows, pigs and geese were herded together into Farmer Buck's transit van (yes, it was a bit of a squeeze, but Farmer Buck didn't care about a little thing like animal welfare) and driven down to the local market where every last creature was swiftly sold to make dog food.

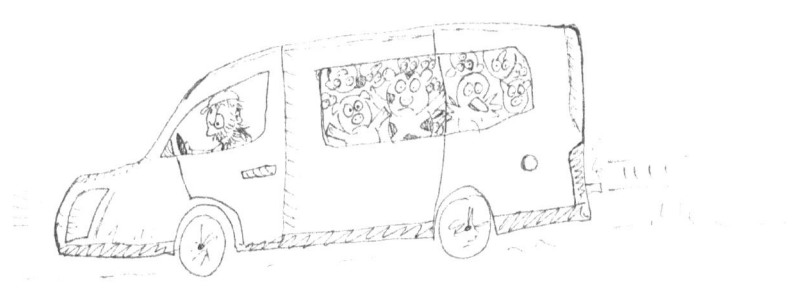

Farmer Buck only kept a few fields, mostly of crops. The cash from the oats and wheat brought in little income for the upkeep of the farm. But Farmer Buck liked money; in fact, he loved money more than life itself, and he had bigger plans for the farm, or at least the land that the farm sat on.

Chapter 2
Making a Quick Buck

Farmer Buck wanted to develop the land he owned into an ultra-exclusive spa resort.

He had plans for the spa to be amazing and one-of-a-kind, equipped with a jacuzzi the size of two swimming pools; indoor, outdoor, heated and music-playing swimming pools, each the size of four swimming pools; a sauna drier and hotter than a Pharaoh's sandal; a steam room steamier than the revolting steamed broccoli that your mum makes you eat; and an ice house colder than Jack Frost's nose.

The surrounding grounds were to be a 25-hole golf course (why have only 18 holes when you can have 25?); double the number of tennis courts as Wimbledon (just to show off); pristine, manicured lawns edged with shrubs from every continent of the world; and ten helipads, as this was the class of client Farmer Buck was looking to attract. I'm not quite sure that Farmer Buck had even been to an airport before because, if he had, he would have known that a real helicopter (or rather ten helicopters) aren't as quiet as the remote controlled helicopters that Pete and Paul played with. The sound of ten helicopters taking off in unison would hardly be the type of noise that you would wish for at an exclusive spa, don't you think?!

Anyway, this spa resort would cost money, a lot more than the money Farmer Buck got for selling his oats and wheat. He had been to all of the local banks with his 'great idea', looking for a loan, but to no avail. If

he had friends he would have thought about asking them for a loan, but unfortunately Farmer Buck wasn't the befriending type, and they probably wouldn't have given him any money anyway.

One day, Farmer Buck and his two sons were sitting around the breakfast table, when Pete and Paul started to tell their father about the internet, and the publicity and attention that campaigns and appeals online get.

'So, Dad, you could have an appeal online, through social media, where you ask for a donation to make you rich overnight, and some folk will pay!' said either Pete or Paul (the one sitting on the right).

'Yeah, you'd get loads of attention. Just say you'll give the money to charity afterwards or something like that,' said the other casually.

Farmer Buck's eyes lit up. 'Could that really work?' he thought.

With his sons' help, by the following week Farmer Buck's appeal website was up and running. 'Make Me a Millionaire Overnight and Help Me Get into the

Guinness Book of Records!' was the title, and through another social media channel he posted a two-minute video of the appeal, where he said he would be giving the money made to charity, which he of course had no such intention of doing.

Five days later, with 1.1 million likes on one social media website and 810,000 views of his video on

another, Farmer Buck's appeal had gone viral. Before long, Farmer Buck was rich. Not quite a millionaire, but rich nonetheless. It had worked. He now had enough money to put his plans into action. He danced around the farmyard for hours that afternoon, strutting around like a crazy crane.

But alas, there was a problem. And that problem was black and white and lived at the bottom of his farm. This might sound like the start of a joke. But trust me, this was no joke. Meet Mr Badger. Or to his friends, who now include you, meet Meles!

Chapter 3
Life Underground for the Badger Family

Meles lived with his wife and their two cubs underneath a hawthorn hedge, at the top of a dry ditch, next to Cuckoo Nest Farm.

Their home wasn't anything special to look at; in fact it was nothing more than two holes, slightly wider than they were tall, which they called 'The Sett'. From the entrance of one of the holes a tunnel passed down deep into the side of the ditch, where, after about two metres, it forked into two, with one of the tunnels passing into one large underground chamber, and the other tunnel passing into a number of smaller interconnected chambers, which themselves were connected to the second hole.

As you might imagine, each chamber was dark, but all chambers were comfortably warm and dry. Furniture was sparse; in fact it was non-existent. However, the floor of the large chamber was covered in a deep thatch of dry grass, which Meles and his wife had collected from outside their home. All four badgers slept and relaxed on this bedding every day. It was so heavily used, in fact, that it had to be replaced with new thatch every few weeks.

Further down the ditch was another hole which Meles sometimes used; they called this hole 'The Outlier'. This one was not connected to The Sett, but it was a convenient resting snug for Meles when his wife's snoring got too bad!

Meles and his family lived the same way as his parents had done before him, and as his grandparents had done before them. The Sett had been in Meles's family for 60 years, having been passed down from father to son. In these 60 years, life had been good. Farmer Buck Senior and Meles had a mutual respect for one another, and the old farmer sometimes even used to put food outside their home, for his black and white friends to scoff for supper.

But, now that the old man had gone and his less accommodating son had taken over Cuckoo Nest Farm, the future wasn't looking as rosy for Meles and his family.

Chapter 4
A Warning for Farmer Buck

Farmer Buck wanted Meles and his family gone. In fact, he wanted all animals on his land gone. He wanted swimming pools, jacuzzis and tennis courts, not fields, hedges and ditches - and definitely not badgers!

So, you might ask, if Farmer Buck and his two gruesome sons hated animals so much, then why did the terrible trio not just dig the badgers out or send Mr Scruff down the hole to chase the black and white squatters away? Well, they did try, but first you have to understand what had happened before Farmer Buck had this 'badger problem'.

Farmer Buck was well-known as a person who treated animals badly. For example, he had superglued a live hedgehog to the ground by his farmhouse's front door, where it was unduly used to scrape the bottom of his, and Pete and Paul's, muddy boots.

He had used a live deer stag, which he had attached with a bungee cord to the wall in his hallway, to hang their hats on.

He had gaffer taped a live squirrel to a wooden pole and used the poor animal's tail to get into those hard-to-reach areas when he dusted (which was hardly ever).

He had trained a magpie to raid the nests of birds, and to bring the eggs and chicks back to him.

He then blitzed them up using a blender and, after adding a splodging of tripe, made a horrible glop which he fed to Mr Scruff for breakfast. The magpie got nothing in return (and they say magpies are intelligent - well not this one!).

He was a useless fisherman, so he trapped a heron and tied it to his fishing rod, which he then used to spear some of the biggest fish you're likely to see.

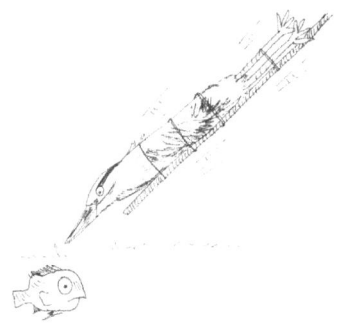

All of these nasty attacks on animals hadn't gone unnoticed. A Royal Society for the Protection of Animals Officer called Jenni Wren and a Wildlife Protection Officer called PC Jack Daws had heard rumours of Farmer Buck's antics. So they had visited Cuckoo Nest Farm and had been welcomed by the hedgehog boot scrubber, even before they had rung the doorbell.

Farmer Buck was told in no uncertain terms that his treatment of animals was totally unacceptable, and that if he was found being cruel towards another animal they would act to close his farm down. This would mean that there would be no way he would get planning consent for the spa. And, with that, Jenni Wren and PC Daws had gone around the house confiscating the animal hostages. This, however, did not stop Farmer Buck trying to pull one more cruel stunt.

Chapter 5
Don't even think about it, Farmer Buck!

Farmer Buck was aware that he was being watched by Jenni Wren and PC Daws for any foul play. He had to tread carefully.

So one day, just as it was getting dark, Farmer Buck armed himself with a torch and a spade and he and Mr Scruff left Cuckoo Nest Farm and walked down to Meles's home. 'It's time to get rid of the black and white vermin,' he had thought.

On reaching the holes, Farmer Buck approached one and shone the torch deep down into the entrance. There was no sign of the badger family.

'Right boy, down you go,' he said, turning to Mr Scruff and bending down to undo his canine friend's leash. As he was doing this there was a rustle of leaves from above. Farmer Buck shot back up and pointed his torch into the tree canopy.

'Good evening, Farmer Buck!' There in the tree, with their heads poking out of the leaves, were Jenni Wren and PC Jack Daws. They both shot down the tree trunk and moved towards Farmer Buck.

'Oh hello Miss Wren ... Officer,' Farmer Buck replied, tipping his head slightly whilst attempting to hide the spade behind his back.

'Can I ask what it is you are doing?' said PC Daws.

'Just out for a quiet walk. Mr Scruff needed his legs stretching.'

'And where does that spade behind your back come into it?'

'Oh this ..." he said, revealing the spade. 'Ehm, I was shifting coal for the fire before, and I clean forgot I still had it. Can you believe that?' Farmer Buck snorted.

'No we can't!' Jenni answered, with a stern look on her face. Farmer Buck gulped.

'If I didn't know better ... or, actually, stuff that ... I do know better. You were going to get rid of Meles and his family tonight, weren't you Farmer Buck?'

'No, no I wasn't!' Farmer Buck lied, badly.

'Listen, pal!' PC Daws barked, staring into Farmer Buck's face. Farmer Buck could see the police officer's nostril twitch and a redness appear in his face, like he was ready to explode. 'If we catch you one more time even thinking about harming an animal we will shut

this farm down before you can say Old Macdonald! Got that?!'

Farmer Buck was going to ask how they would know that he was 'thinking about harming an animal', but he thought better of it. PC Daws didn't look like he was taking questions. The police officer's face was now redder than Santa Claus's nose.

'Do I make myself clear?!' he boomed. Even Jenni Wren looked a little scared, and she was on PC Daws's side!

'Yes, of course, Officer.'

'Good night then,' PC Daws said, moving away and scooting back up the tree again, with Jenni Wren following.

Farmer Buck and Mr Scruff turned and started to head back to the farmhouse. Farmer Buck pondered. Were they guarding Meles's home? More importantly, what were they doing on his land ... and up a tree?! And could he order a police officer off his land? Regardless of the answers, Farmer Buck was well and truly under surveillance, so, if he wanted rid of Meles and the rest of the badgers, he would have to play fair and keep within the law, or he risked losing everything. By the time they reached the front door of his farmhouse, he had just the idea.

Chapter 6
A Proposition for Meles

The following day Farmer Buck made a telephone call to a man about a digger. It is common knowledge that badgers are good diggers. Well, Farmer Buck had a proposition for Meles, and that proposition was a digging competition. Farmer Buck had enlisted an old acquaintance called Doug and his 21-tonne digger, which came with Douglas, a complementary banksman, whose job was to stand with his hands in his pockets watching the digger dig, occasionally warning Doug that he was about to crash into something, or someone.

Farmer Buck was going to challenge Meles to a digging contest, the winner being whoever dug deepest - Doug's digger or the badger. The prizes were simple. If the digger won, Meles and his family would have to leave the ditch and Cuckoo Nest Farm for good; the emphasis of course being on 'good'. If Meles won, his badger family could stay in their home and Farmer Buck would ensure that there would be a plentiful supply of wheat and oats in the fields for them for evermore.

Even though Farmer Buck knew that badgers dug well, he was absolutely certain that the digger would easily out-dig Meles, who would, he guessed, be exhausted after an hour or so. This was a safe bet, so long as Meles was daft enough to agree to it.

So, at lunchtime, Farmer Buck walked down to the badger sett and knelt down outside one of the holes.

'Hello, hellllloooo Meles!' he called down the hole.

'Sorry to wake you. Do you have a minute, my friend?'

Just then, Farmer Buck noticed movement in the hole. Meles's sleepy head gradually came into view. His eyes squinted in the sunlight.

'How can I help you, Farmer Buck?' he asked suspiciously, looking up at the little man kneeling at the entrance to his house.

'Yes, sorry to bother you, but just a quick one, neighbour. I have always thought of you as someone who likes a challenge. You know, determined ... persistent.' Farmer Buck turned to the side and rolled his eyes.

'OK,' Meles said hesitantly.

'Well, I have a contest that may interest you.'

Farmer Buck told Meles about the digger, the contest, and what was at stake, if he was game.

After a moment thinking, Meles replied, 'Yes, OK. Why not.'

'Sorry?' Farmer Buck thought that he had misheard.

'Yes, I'm happy to challenge the digger. And you say that my family and I will stay here if I win, and you'll make sure there's always wheat and oats for us to fill our tummies with?' he said.

'Yes, yes, more wheat and oats than you could possibly fit in your tummies!' Farmer Buck exclaimed.

The farmer felt excitement bubbling up inside him. This was going to be easy, like taking candy off a kid. Or, rather, taking wheat off a badger. Farmer Buck's mind was wandering to a life free of Meles. As soon as he and his pitiful family were gone, he'd bulldoze the whole ditch, hedge and fields. Everything! The badger home would be flattened. Ground to a pulp. Reduced to dust. However you like to say it, Meles's home would be a home no more.

Farmer Buck had to be absolutely certain that he was going to win, so he added, 'I appreciate that you're a wonderful digger … so I wonder whether you would agree to me and my sons also digging against you as part of the contest?'

'Yes, why not. The more the merrier,' Meles said cheerily. 'In fact, that scraggy dog of yours could dig against me too if you wanted?'

Farmer Buck felt a sudden rage rise up in his core, like lava in a volcano ready to erupt. 'I'll give you a scraggy dog,' he thought.

'Wonderful idea,' Farmer Buck said with a forced grin. 'How are you placed for this evening for the contest? Say nine?'

'Tonight at nine is as good a time as any. See you then, Farmer Buck,' Meles said with a chirp, and he disappeared back into the darkness of his hole.

Farmer Buck joyously jogged his way back to his farmhouse; it was time to rally the troops.

Chapter 7
Contenders Ready?

At nine o'clock, Farmer Buck, Pete and Paul, Mr Scruff and the digger, with Doug inside and Douglas outside, arrived outside Meles's house. The badger appeared from the hole. As he looked around he was faced with four angry faces, one snaring face and one smiling face - Farmer Buck. Meles was starting to get slightly worried by Farmer Buck's new-found pleasantness. In fact, his smiling face was more disturbing than the unpleasant faces of the others. Why was the farmer suddenly being so nice to him?

'Good evening, Meles. What a fine night for it.' smirked Farmer Buck.

'Yes, I was thinking the very same thing.'

'I suggest that the contest takes place in the field of set-aside, across here,' Farmer Buck said, pointing his torch over an adjacent hedge. 'We don't want to damage the oats or wheat, do we now?'

'Yes of course,' the badger said, walking behind the other contenders who moved slowly through the field of wheat.

'Will your family be watching the contest tonight my friend?' Farmer Buck asked over his shoulder.

'I've not actually told them about this. I didn't want to worry them.'

Farmer Buck couldn't help but smile. He would be more than happy to be the bearer of the bad news to

Meles's wife that her hopeless husband had fairly lost a digging competition, and that they and their horrible cubs would be evicted from their home quick smart as a result. This was going to be an even more enjoyable evening than he had originally thought. He gave a little hop of pleasure.

The group passed through a gap in a hedge and into the next field, with Farmer Buck and Mr Scruff leading the way, Pete and Paul next, followed by Douglas and Doug with the digger, and Meles walking at the back. The headlights of the digger illuminated the way. Farmer Buck came to a halt.

'OK, we should all spread out. Doug, you guys go over there. Mr Scruff can dig there. Me and the boys can dig here, and you, Meles, can dig there,' Farmer Buck said, pointing in various directions. The contenders spaced out.

Doug sat in the cabin of his digger; his head almost touched the roof, he was so tall. Douglas stood outside; he was about as tall as Doug. Doug and Douglas were so tall they were sometimes paid by the local school

to stand with one hand touching and the other hand vertical, to act as one of the goals during rugby matches. The pair would do anything if there was some cash on offer.

Douglas stood by the digger and gave the thumbs up to Doug, who sat in the cabin. The digger's headlights illuminated the ground in front, where Doug would be digging. Mr Scruff sat looking at Farmer Buck, ready for the order to dig. Farmer Buck stood with a spade in his hand, and Pete and Paul by his side. Meles crouched and cracked his paws, staring at Farmer Buck with a look of steely determination.

Farmer Buck thought, 'It's no good, my friend. You don't have a snowball's chance of winning!'

'Right boys. Pete - I want you to stand here and shine this torch so I can see what I'm doing. Paul - you stand with this torch and shine it over by Mr Scruff!' Farmer Buck ordered. 'We can swap places when I'm knackered. OK, everyone - are we all set?'

Altogether, the contenders shouted 'YES!'

'In that case, READY, STEADY, DIG!!'

Chapter 8
Off like a Greased Ferret

The four contenders started to dig madly. Farmer Buck wildly threw the spade into the earth. Mr Scruff scraped away at the ground, as if digging for his favourite bone. Doug manoeuvred the digger bucket so it excavated a huge block of earth, which he quickly dropped to the side. And, finally, there was Meles, who relatively slowly, but methodologically, shovelled the earth with his large clawed paws.

After thirty minutes Doug was well in the lead and had dug down about two metres, much more than the others. Farmer Buck was next deepest, followed by Mr Scruff and Meles, who were about neck and neck. Farmer Buck straightened up and wiped the sweat from his brow.

Just then a cat appeared by the hedge at the side of the field. Instantly Mr Scruff got the scent. He threw his head up and his wet nose wriggled around frantically in the air; his nostrils were filled with the unmistakable smell of cat. Mr Scruff couldn't help himself. He shot off like a greased ferret towards the cat, which, unsurprisingly, turned and darted away. Farmer Buck saw a flash in front of him as Mr Scruff zoomed past.

'Wait, Mr Scruff!' Farmer Buck cried, throwing his hands in the air and dropping the spade to the ground. But it was no good; Mr Scruff was on a mission. And that mission did not now concern a digging contest against a badger. He was off. The cat disappeared along the hedge into the night, followed by Mr Scruff. Farmer Buck had lost one of his team.

Chapter 9
A Cracking Effort, Farmer Buck

'Stupid thing!' barked Farmer Buck.

'Right, your turn, Pete,' he ordered, grabbing the torch off the boy and pointing towards the spade. Pete picked it up and started to thrust it into the earth.

Paul walked over to his father. 'Dad, don't worry. The digger's winning by a mile anyway. That stupid badger's got no chance. Look, he's knackered!' Paul shone the torch across to Meles's pit. Indeed, the badger looked as though he was having a break. He was sitting in the pit he had dug, and Farmer Buck could only see his head and shoulders, which were still.

'Everything OK, Meles? Are you finished?' Farmer Buck called across with a smile.

'Everything's fine, Farmer Buck. I'm just having a little break. I see you've lost a team member though?' he responded.

'He was dead wood anyway. He was almost doing as badly as you, my friend!' Farmer Buck shouted.

After another thirty minutes Doug was well ahead, about three metres deeper than Meles. The Bucks were starting to fall behind.

'Right, my turn again!' Farmer Buck yelled, rushing forward and grabbing the spade off Pete. 'We're last, thanks to you! Look, you can't see the badger now - he's that deep!'

Farmer Buck threw the blade of the spade into the

ground. 'Come on, must go quicker!' he screamed, like a mad man. After ten wild thrusts of the spade into the ground there was an almighty SNAAAAAAAAP!

'What was that noise?!' he shouted, as the spade splintered and the handle and around thirty centimetres of the top of the stem came away in his hand, leaving the rest of the spade still firmly in the ground. 'Blasted thing!' he yelled and he threw the top half of the spade like a javelin across the field. Farmer Buck slumped down into the pit he had dug and put his head in his hands.

'Dad, Dad, remember the digger!' Pete said. 'It's still winning!'

In his panic, Farmer Buck had almost forgotten about the digger, which he now couldn't see as it was so deep in its excavation.

'Of course!' he cried, grabbing the torch and rushing across to where Douglas stood at the edge of the pit. Pete and Paul hastily followed.

Chapter 10
Working Night and Day

When they got to the edge of the pit they took a look in; the digger was about five and a half metres down. Farmer Buck quickly rushed across to Meles's excavation and looked in. He guessed that the badger was about two and a half metres down. 'Well behind,' he thought, smiling.

The contest went on and on. Midnight came and went. Then one o'clock, then two o'clock, then three o'clock. The digger and Meles had been digging for over six hours!

The digger was now about twenty metres deep, with the badger still behind at about ten metres. A terrific depth for such an animal to dig, but he was losing nonetheless. Farmer Buck was running frantically between both pits to make sure that the badger was still losing.

Suddenly, Farmer Buck had a thought. It was almost four o'clock and sunrise was only thirty minutes away. There would be no way that Meles would be out in broad daylight, so, if Doug could just keep going and stay in front of the badger for another half hour, he was pretty sure the animal would stop and the contest would finally be over. And, finally, the badgers would have to go once and for all!

After a little time, the sun poked its head out from the hill-tops. Farmer Buck hopped across to Meles's pit and called down smugly.

'Getting light, isn't it, my old mate? Not your cup of tea, is it, my friend?'

'I don't know, Farmer. It's not getting light way down here anyway,' Meles called back over his shoulder, as he continued to dig at the soil at the bottom of the pit.

'Damn, damn,' Farmer Buck scolded under his breath. Of course, the sunlight wouldn't get down to Meles. It was as good as night for him down there in the pit. Farmer Buck slammed a foot down onto the ground and watched the determined animal continue to rake at the soil with his powerful paws.

After a few minutes, Farmer Buck turned back around and could just make out the figures of Pete, Paul and Douglas, who were now lying on the ground in a heap. He could hear their ghastly snoring all the way from where he was standing. They sounded like the laziest choir in the world.

However, what was more troubling was that he could no longer hear the soft drone of the digger as he moved closer to the edge of Doug's pit.

Chapter 11
Sleeping on the Job

When Farmer Buck looked down he saw that the digger was stationary.

'Doug! Doug!' he shouted. 'Are you asleep man?!'

There was no answer. Just then, he heard an almighty snort, like a pig, from the depths of the pit. Doug's snoring echoed all the way up the sides of the hole. That answered his question! He was going to have to get down there. He needed rope. There was some in one of his barns back at the farm he thought, and he looked at Pete and Paul. They were sound asleep.

'Oh, I'll do it myself!' he snapped, storming back towards his farm.

After a few minutes he returned with a long length of rope. He had a quick look into Meles's pit. The creature was still digging. When he got back to the edge of the digger's pit he realised that the depths were almost neck and neck! He started to panic.

'Wake up you daft galoots!' he shouted, kicking Pete and Paul's boots. 'Come quick, the badger's almost winning!'

The two boys got to their feet gingerly and followed their father to the edge of the pit.

'Right, both of you hold this and lower me down!' yelled Farmer Buck, handing one end of the rope to Paul and tying the other end around his waist.

'Why, Dad, what's happened?'

'I need to go down there because the digger's not digging, and Doug's sleeping like a baby!'

From the edge of the pit the two boys lowered their lightweight father down, with Paul holding the end of the rope and Pete feeding it gradually through his fingers.

After what seemed like an eternity, Farmer Buck landed onto the roof of the digger. He untied the rope from his waist.

'Right boys, I'm down!' he called up.

'Doug! Wake up!'

Farmer Buck clambered onto the back wheel of the digger and then moved around to the front, where he was greeted by Doug's face pressed against the side window. He was sleeping soundly.

'Doug! Wake up!' Farmer Buck shouted again, and he opened the side door. Doug started to fall out. 'Doug! Doug!'

The digger driver just mumbled something about his digger being bigger than the rest, so Farmer Buck took matters into his own hands.

'Right, get out, you!' With some difficulty, he pulled the sleeping giant out and dumped him onto the ground at the side of the digger. Doug didn't even stir as he landed with a thud. Farmer Buck climbed into the driver's seat of the digger and took hold of the levers, which he just about could reach.

'OK, time to be beaten once and for all, Meles!' he shouted, as the digger bucket crunched into the ground.

Another two hours passed with Farmer Buck frantically digging against the equally determined Meles. Farmer Buck had taken a slight lead.

'Dad, you're leading!' came a yell from above. Pete and Paul were rushing between the two pits and giving their father a running commentary.

'Is that badger still digging?' he yelled back up.

'Yeah, he is!'

Farmer Buck shook his head in amazement.

'Time to finish this contest off once and for all!'

Chapter 12
The Flames of Hell

Farmer Buck started to thrust the lever of the digger roughly into the earth. All of a sudden, the digger engine started to slow, stall and stutter.

'Boys, get more diesel!' he called up. 'I think it's running out!'

Pete turned around and rushed back towards the farmhouse. Minutes later he arrived back with a jerry can full of fuel.

'Dad! Dad! DAAAAAAAAAD!' Pete screamed down into the pit. Farmer Buck looked up out of the digger, which had now cut out.

'Right, Pete, throw it down. But make sure you keep it that side,' Farmer Buck called, looking up at Pete and pointing to the far side of the pit. 'I don't want to be hit by that thing. It'll kill me!'

'OK, here it comes, Dad!' Pete launched the jerry can into the abyss. It flew through the air for a few seconds, before hitting the bottom of the pit with a clang.

'Right, one of you go and check what that badger is doing!' Farmer Buck called up.

Paul ran across to the other pit, whilst Farmer Buck searched for the fuel cap on the digger, using a small torch which he'd taken from his pocket. He found it on the side of the machine, poured the diesel in and tossed the empty can to the side.

'Dad…' came a voice from above.

'Yes?!' Farmer Buck shouted back.

'I think the badger is in the lead again! I can hardly see him, he's that deep!'

'Damn it!' Farmer Buck hurried into the digger's cabin and turned the key. It spluttered and the engine started, but it sounded different from before. He ignored that fact, grabbed the lever and thrust the digger's bucket forward.

He dug madly, with the bucket getting faster and faster, but the engine got more and more rattly. Farmer Buck was so focused on the digging that he didn't notice the smoke start to seep from the engine at the rear of the digger. However, by the time it was spewing out of the engine, he noticed all right. The smoke was now engulfing the pit.

'Arghhh!' he screamed. 'HELP!'

He shot out of the cabin like he had been fired out of a cannon.

'BOYS! The digger's going to blow! The rope! Pull up the rope!'

He ran across to the rope, which jolted up just before he got there.

'Not yet! Wait until I'm holding it!' he screamed.

He spluttered as he inhaled some of the smoke. The rope dropped down a little so Farmer Buck could grab it. He covered his mouth and waved his other hand in front of his face to try and flap the smoke away.

As he grabbed hold of the rope there was a loud bang and flames started to fan out from the engine box. Farmer Buck saw some movement to the side of the stricken digger. It was the figure of Doug, slowly getting to his substantial feet. Farmer Buck had forgotten about the sleeping giant who had been collapsed in a heap all this time.

'Oh, so something could wake you then?!' Farmer Buck snapped. 'Grab the rope you big oaf. Quick, otherwise we're both going to be burnt to a crisp!'

Doug stumbled across to Farmer Buck, and grabbed hold of the rope.

'Right boys, bring us up. And quick!' Farmer Buck screamed.

The rope tightened and gradually both men were slowly lifted from the pit floor. Pete, Paul, and the now-awake Douglas pulled and pulled with all their might, as the rope strained under Farmer Buck and Doug's weight.

Meles had won the digging contest and Farmer Buck had lost. But now Farmer Buck had another battle; this time, to save himself!

Chapter 13
A Sore Loser

Farmer Buck could feel the heat from the burning digger, which now resembled a bonfire, on the back of his neck. However, this was no time to roast any marshmallows. He had to get out of this pit of hell before he and Doug were blown into next week, or indeed the week after that.

Doug was swinging from the rope, underneath Farmer Buck. Farmer Buck had made sure that he had clambered above the dozy sod, so that, if the farmer did slip, at least his landing would be soft, being Doug's head!

The flames rose from the bottom of the pit like a group of dancing serpents coming out of a snake charmer's basket. Doug's boots were starting to melt. The soles were dripping like melting ice lollies.

'Hurry! We're going to be toast!' Farmer Buck cried, as he shut his eyes and slowly climbed the rope a little further.

They were about ten metres from the surface of the ground, when suddenly there was an almighty 'BOOM!'

from below. The digger had blown up. Actually, to be precise, the digger's engine had blown up. Farmer Buck felt a rush of hot air, flames and mechanical debris pushing up from beneath him. Suddenly Doug flew up, and was higher than him. The force of the explosion shot both men clean out of the pit, and as high as a double-decker bus into the air.

Pete, Paul and Douglas were thrown back by the sudden force of the eruption. It all happened so quickly, like a spurting geyser. Farmer Buck landed on a hedge way across to the side of the field, and Doug landed straight into a nearby ditch, with a SPLODGE!

'Dad, Dad, you OK?' the boys shouted in unison, rushing across to their father, who was hanging crumpled in the hawthorn. Douglas ran across to see his pal, Doug, who was now face down in umpteen inches of thick mud.

When Pete and Paul got to their father he was wriggling about and trying to climb down from the spiky bush. The small man looked like the most unhappy and unwilling angel on top of a cheap, unkempt Christmas tree.

The boys helped him onto the ground. Farmer Buck's face was black as night with the smoke dust, and his clothes were ripped like they had been through a paper shredder.

'That absolutely does it!' Farmer Buck boomed, dusting himself down.

Pete and Paul were going to say to their father that he had something on his face, but they thought better of it. The farmer marched across to the pit Meles was still digging in. Pete and Paul looked at each other, and then hastily followed their fuming father. Farmer Buck stopped at the edge of the pit and looked down.

'Give me that torch!' He snatched the torch from Pete, switched it on, and pointed the light deep down into the pit. He could just make out the back of a badger, metres and metres below. The creature appeared to be digging still. Even from this elevated point Farmer Buck could clearly see that he had dug deeper than anyone and had therefore won the contest. But Farmer Buck was a sore loser and poor Meles was about to find this out.

Chapter 14
The Only Way Is Up

'OK, you've won, Meles!' Farmer Buck yelled down into the pit. The badger stopped and looked up. 'It is a pity, though, that you won't be around to get your prize!' Farmer Buck gave a chuckle, and threw the torch to the ground. 'Goodbye my friend.'

With that, he picked up a large block of excavated earth next to him and tossed it straight into the pit.

Meles put his arms above his head, protecting himself from the raining earth and stones. Farmer Buck was going to bury him alive! He had to get out and fast! He thought about digging sideways out of the pit, but it would be difficult, if not impossible, to then dig upwards through compacted ground. No, his best bet was to clamber up the pit wall. Badgers were good climbers, and Meles was no exception. More debris rained down on him. Meles placed his paws onto the pit wall, and heaved himself up.

Meanwhile, up above, Pete and Paul had joined their father in hurling earth and other debris down into the pit.

Just then, Farmer Buck heard a loud cough from behind him. He swung around to see Jenni Wren clamber out of a nearby dry ditch, and PC Daws appear from a cavity in a large oak tree at the side of the field.

'Good morning, Farmer Buck,' PC Daws said merrily.

'Is it?' Farmer Buck replied, throwing the block of earth in his hands to the ground. Pete and Paul took a step back from the pit edge.

'If our ears weren't deceiving us, you had a bet with Meles that he could stay in his home if he won the digging contest. Is that correct?' Jenni Wren asked, as she walked towards Farmer Buck.

'Yes,' Farmer Buck answered, reluctantly.

'And if, we're not mistaken, he did win, did he not?'

Farmer Buck was not quite sure where the RSPCA officer and police constable had been all this time, but it was obvious that they had seen and heard everything. He nodded.

'Then tell me this, Farmer Buck. Why are you trying to bury poor Meles alive? That wasn't his prize now, was it?!' PC Daws barked.

'No, Officer.' Farmer Buck bowed his head and slumped to the ground.

'Now, as we are all fair creatures, and I'm sure you, Farmer Buck are a man of your word—' Jenni Wren started, before being interrupted by PC Daws.

'Put it this way, Farmer Buck. You're going to be jailed and fined, and your farm will be taken off you, if you don't treat Meles well and keep to your promise that he and his family can stay!'

It was that simple; the badgers were staying, otherwise Farmer Buck was to lose everything. But this meant that he could not build his dream money-making spa.

'Officers, I don't suppose your viewpoint could be swayed slightly ... you know, financially?' Farmer Buck said hesitantly. It was worth a try.

'You should be aware, Farmer Buck, that attempting to bribe a police officer is an offence and is considered a very serious matter. I suggest you retract that statement,' said PC Daws.

'Statement retracted,' Farmer Buck replied, glumly.

Just then there was a scraping noise from the pit. They all turned around to see Meles's head appear at the top.

'So I won?' he said with a smile.

Farmer Buck put his head in his hands.

Chapter 15
A Second Proposition for Meles

PC Daws and Jenni Wren looked at Farmer Buck. He lifted his head out of his hands.

'Yes, you did. You dug well,' Farmer Buck said. He could hardly look at the victor.

PC Daws and Jenni Wren went across and helped Meles out of the pit. He shook to get the dust and dirt off of himself.

'I thought you were going to bury me alive there at one point,' the badger said.

'Ehm...' Farmer Buck thought about how he should respond.

'It was just a moment of madness, wasn't it, Farmer Buck? But it definitely won't happen again, will it?' PC Daws prompted, with his glaring eyes firming on the farmer.

'Yes, yes. I mean no, no it won't happen again, of course not,' Farmer Buck flustered, his thoughts suddenly turning to his dwindling spa plans. He just had to get rid of the badgers. He was not willing to give up on his dream. He could almost touch the spa and the money it would make!

'I say, you're a fair and courageous badger, Meles,' Farmer Buck propositioned, composing himself.

'I like to think I'm fair, yes, Farmer Buck.'

Farmer Buck collected his thoughts.

'I wonder, in that case, whether you would be interested in a final challenge. One final contest?'

'I'm listening,' the badger replied.

Jenni Wren and PC Daws, and Pete and Paul, were all listening intently.

'I challenged you before to the digging contest with the sole goal of beating you, so that you had to move off my land.'

'Yes.'

'Well, obviously you won. So you can stay, and you can help yourself to my cereal crops. However,' Farmer Buck continued, 'I wonder whether you would be brave enough to risk staying here for a double prize if you win. Double or quits if you like. The quits part is that you would quit living here.'

'And what's the double prize?' Meles asked.

'Well, if you win, we swap houses. You and your family will live in my farmhouse and we' —Farmer Buck gestured towards Pete and Paul— 'will live in your foul hole.'

Pete and Paul looked at their father in horror, but Farmer Buck knew that he had to pull out all the stops.

'OK sounds tempting. And the challenge?' asked the badger.

'Well, Meles,' Farmer Buck started. 'I have noticed that you are partial to wheat, judging by the amount of crop that I lose every year around here?'

The badger did not say anything, but he kept looking at Farmer Buck.

'Well, the challenge I propose is a harvest contest. Each of us has one field of wheat, and the winner is the one who harvests their field the quickest. I will use my 16-tonne combine harvester as I always do, and you, my friend, your good old-fashioned claws and paws. What do you say? I know you like a challenge, my friend.'

The badger looked away, deep in thought.

'Don't feel that you have to, Meles,' Jenni Wren said. But Meles did indeed enjoy a challenge, and the prospect of him and his family living in the lovely, spacious farmhouse was hard to ignore. As was the prospect of the farmer and his horrible sons being squeezed into their underground home.

'I accept your challenge, Farmer Buck. How does tonight sound?'

'Yes, of course, great,' smirked Farmer Buck. There was no chance of Meles winning this time. His combine harvester harvested a width of around ten metres of crop with every slight movement forward, and the badger could only cut, say, one metre at a time. This would definitely be easy!

'Having the contest tonight means that, out of

courtesy, I have time to dig out my home, to make it a little more spacious for you and your boys after I win,' Meles said.

'Ha-ha, no need my friend. I doubt you will have any chance. But, very well. I will see you back here at nine o'clock and we can get started.'

And, with that, Farmer Buck and his two boys turned and headed back towards the farmhouse. Meles rushed back to his home; he had work to do.

Chapter 16
A Mechanical Monster

For the rest of the afternoon and early evening Meles dug his house even deeper and wider. He made it about twice as deep and twice as wide.

He told his wife about the contest.

'My love, you have no chance of winning,' she replied 'Have you seen the size of his combine harvester blades? He'll have the field cut in less than an hour, even before you've done one strip.'

'Don't worry, my dear, I have a plan.' And, with that, Meles gave his wife a little reassuring wink.

'I do hope you know what you're doing.'

That evening, Meles stood at the edge of the field where his home was, waiting for Farmer Buck to arrive. He had told his wife to take their two young ones out for a meal in the local woodland as normal. He was not keen on them watching the contest, as he thought it would make him quite jittery.

The quiet of the night was broken by the distant sound of a vehicle on the track down from Cuckoo Nest farmhouse. Meles could see the headlights of a monstrous vehicle; it was crawling slowly. After ten minutes, the combine harvester pulled up in front of him, with Farmer Buck behind the large steering wheel.

Farmer Buck killed the engine and opened the cabin door. He went down the steps which descended from the cabin and jumped onto the ground. The combine

harvester was truly enormous. Coming face to face with the mechanical beast, Meles felt small and weak. He tried to look confident, but he was beginning to wonder whether he had made a wise decision with this contest.

'Good evening, Meles. Another fine night,' Farmer Buck called chirpily.

'Yes indeed,' the badger replied.

'OK, seeing as how you have next to no chance of winning, old boy, I will let you choose which field of wheat you want to clear,' Farmer Buck said.

'This one,' the farmer said, pointing to the field which contained Meles's home along its edge, 'or this one?' He gestured over to another field of wheat.

'I will go into the field over here,' Meles said, indicating the neighbouring wheat field, 'if that's OK?'

'OK, so be it. I will clear this wheat then. Good, good, my old pal.'

Farmer Buck turned around and climbed up the steps back into the combine harvester's cabin, followed by Pete and Paul.

'Get into your starting position. I will sound my horn to begin!' he shouted, before closing the cabin door.

Meles cracked his paws as he moved into the neighbouring wheat field and got into position. For both Meles and Farmer Buck, this was a battle for all, or nothing.

Chapter 17
The End Is In Sight

Farmer Buck watched Meles pass through a gap in the perimeter hedge and stop in the corner of the adjacent wheat field. He sounded the horn of the combine harvester. The harvest race had begun!

The badger thrashed at the wheat with his strong paws. Stems of wheat plants threw through the air in all directions. He moved slowly forwards, as the crop gradually began to be cleared.

Meanwhile, in the other field, Farmer Buck was moving the combine harvester. Metres and metres of wheat were being cut with every slight forward movement of the machine. After forty minutes the combine harvester was well ahead.

'Dad, you should slow down a bit so he thinks he's got a chance,' Pete suggested.

'Prolong the agony. You're miles ahead,' Paul added.

'Yes, OK, why not?' Farmer Buck replied, looking over at the other wheat field. He stopped the monstrous harvester and turned its engine off. He had only about a third of the field left to clear and he was ready for a rest.

'Just for five minutes though.' Farmer Buck took out a flask of coffee and a Tatler magazine and put his feet up on the steering wheel. Pete and Paul each took out a computer tablet and sat engrossed.

Meles, meanwhile, had a long way to go before he caught up with the combine harvester.

After a few minutes of slurping coffee and reading, Farmer Buck put the lid on his flask and the magazine back under his seat.

'Right, let's finish this job now,' he said, looking at Pete, then Paul, and then turning the key in the ignition. The combine harvester rumbled into action and moved forwards, flattening the wheat as it went.

After two more lengths of the field Farmer Buck only had one final strip to do, then the field would be completely clear of standing crop.

'Look, look at the badger. What's he doing?!' Pete asked, suddenly pointing to Meles who was standing at the edge of their field, illuminated by the combine harvester's headlights.

'Is he finished?' Paul shouted.

Farmer Buck looked into the adjacent field, where around half of the wheat was still standing.

'No, don't be stupid. He must know that he's going to lose and that there's no point in him keeping going. The marvellous Meles has given up!' Farmer Buck yelled with pleasure. He waved at the badger sarcastically.

The stupid creature actually waved back at him.

'Daft animal,' he smirked, moving the combine harvester forward. The harvest race was soon to be over. And Meles knew that too.

Chapter 18
An Earth-shattering Contest

Farmer Buck only had another fifty metre strip to clear and then he would be finished.

'Right, Meles, watch and weep!'

As the combine harvester moved forwards, Farmer Buck felt a massive shudder. Pete and Paul stumbled forwards from their seats. Farmer Buck firmly held onto the steering wheel. All of a sudden, they felt the ground shake violently around them.

'Is it an earthquake?' Pete shouted, as the combine harvester lurched forwards. But Farmer Buck did not have time to answer. The ground gave way beneath them and the mechanical monster crashed forwards and downwards.

CRRRRAAAAASSSHHHHHH!

It was only when the combine harvester came to rest with a jolt that Farmer Buck saw the large underground chamber, and some of the dry bedding scattered over the ground, illuminated by the headlights. It was Meles's home!

Farmer Buck grabbed hold of the door handle and tried to push the door open. But it was stuck fast, as was the other door. Earth and other debris had fallen around the sides of the combine harvester, enclosing Farmer Buck, Pete and Paul.

'We're stuck!' Farmer Buck shouted.

Meles smiled and returned to his field and, after another couple of hours, he finished clearing the wheat. He had won again!

Chapter 19
The Bucks's Downsize

Farmer Buck had been trying to kick open one of the side doors, and Pete and Paul were trying to do the same to the other door, but it was no good. Just then, Farmer Buck saw the earth starting to move through the glass outside his side door. Then he saw a hairy paw appear, and then another. The earth was scraped away from the door and Meles's face came into view. After five minutes, the badger had scraped all of the earth from around the door and Farmer Buck, and Pete and Paul, climbed out of the stranded combine harvester slowly - deflated, defeated and dejected.

It was forty minutes before sunrise, but light was beginning to illuminate the morning sky. Farmer Buck looked across at the fully-cleared field beside his one. The game was up. As Farmer Buck stood next to Meles, he suddenly had a thought. Why did he have to swap houses? After all, he was a man, and Meles was ... well ... a foul creature who lived in the dirt. He put his hand in his pocket and tightly clutched hold of the keys to the farmhouse. He would not give them up.

'Right, Farmer Buck, as I'm sure you're a fair man - despite the image you portray - you and Meles here had a deal,' PC Daws said, suddenly appearing from behind them. Jenni Wren walked beside him, and they both looked directly at Farmer Buck.

'The farmhouse keys, please,' he added, walking over to Farmer Buck and putting out his hand. Farmer Buck was holding the keys in his pocket so tightly it almost hurt. Reluctantly, he brought the keys out and handed them to PC Daws.

'Thank you Farmer Buck; or is it just Mr Buck now?'

PC Daws did not wait for an answer; he walked purposely across to the badger and dropped the keys into his paw. By this time, Meles's wife and his little ones had arrived.

'What's happened?' she asked in shock, staring at their collapsed home, which now had a 16-tonne combine harvester sprouting out of the top of it.

'There was a bit of an accident, my love, but don't worry, it's been sorted,' Meles said, smiling. He showed his wife the keys to the farmhouse in his hand and put his arm around her.

Ex-farmer Buck, and Pete and Paul, turned and looked in horror at their new home. All three stood quietly, with arms straight down at their sides, and with their jaws almost touching the wheat crop that still stood below them.

'It was a pleasure doing business with you, Mr Buck,' Meles said, stepping forward and offering his paw. Ex-farmer Buck turned around and looked down at the badger; he did not respond. His face was in a constant  state of shock, as if he had just witnessed a cataclysmic event, like the end of the world, or just seen a live dinosaur. He did not shake Meles's paw.

'Very well,' Meles said retracting his paw. 'I'm no expert, Mr Buck, but I think you may need your roof fixed.' And, with that, the badger family turned and walked up the track towards Cuckoo Nest farmhouse; their new home.

THE END

Dr Colin Bonnington

Colin works as an ecological consultant based in Manchester. He writes and illustrates wildlife themed stories based on his experiences during his work. He completed a doctorate at the University of Sheffield on the impact of grey squirrels on birds, and still regularly writes scientific journal articles. *Meles and the Ferocious Farmer* is his second book for children. Colin lives in Cheshire with his cat and his wife (and at the moment, her baby bump!).

www.ingramcontent.com/pod-product-compliance
Lightning Source LLC
Chambersburg PA
CBHW050045080526
44586CB00014B/1470